The Angels of Christmas
LEADER GUIDE

The Angels of Christmas
Hearing God's Voice in Advent

The Angels of Christmas
978-1-7910-2425-3
978-1-7910-2426-0 eBook

The Angels of Christmas DVD
978-1-7910-2429-1

The Angels of Christmas Leader Guide
978-1-7910-2427-7
978-1-7910-2428-4 eBook

Also by Susan Robb

Called: Hearing and Responding to God's Voice

Seven Words: Listening to Christ from the Cross

SUSAN ROBB

The Angels of Christmas

HEARING GOD'S VOICE IN ADVENT

LEADER GUIDE
by Randy Horick

Abingdon Press | Nashville

THE ANGELS OF CHRISTMAS
HEARING GOD'S VOICE IN ADVENT
LEADER GUIDE

978-1-7910-2427-7

MANUFACTURED IN THE UNITED STATES OF AMERICA

CONTENTS

INTRODUCTION

No Christmas pageant or Nativity scene is complete without angels. We would never leave them out of any telling of the story of the birth of Jesus. Angels also have become not only familiar but beloved figures in popular culture. In movies and TV shows, they act as guardians who help human beings along the way and, by their reassuring presence, remind us that God is always with us, watching over us.

Precisely because of their familiarity, we may believe we know quite a bit about angels and their role in the Christmas story. We may not take the time to look much beyond their traditional depiction in just one part of that story—a heavenly army announcing Jesus's birth to an astonished group of shepherds in the middle of the night.

In fact, angels serve as messengers to all the main participants in the events leading up to Jesus's birth. They come separately to Elizabeth and Zechariah, the future parents of John the Baptizer, telling the long-childless couple of what God is about to do in their lives—and for the life of the nation. An angel comes to Mary to tell her that she, a teenaged girl in an out-of-the-way village, has been "overshadowed" by God's spirit and will deliver a child who will be the messiah. An angel appears to Joseph, who has been troubled by his betrothed's out-of-wedlock pregnancy, and assures him that Mary's incredible-sounding story is true. And finally, a host of angels illuminate the night sky and tell the shepherds where they can find this newborn baby who represents the Savior of the world.

In *The Angels of Christmas*, Susan Robb invites us to look more deeply at each of these encounters with God's messengers. She examines the lives and experiences of Elizabeth, Zechariah, Mary, Joseph, and the shepherds to better understand how they would have perceived the angels' messages. To deepen our insights, she helps us connect their stories to other figures in biblical history who encountered angels or received astonishing news from God—from Abraham and Sarah to childless and despondent Hannah to doubtful Gideon to the prophet Elijah, who heard God's voice in the middle of silence. Then she explores how these individuals responded to the messages they had heard.

Christmas pageants generally present a unified narrative about the birth of Jesus, complete with the Holy Family, angels, shepherds, wise men, stable animals, and an innkeeper. But only two of the four Gospels even tell the story of Jesus's birth, and each of these two, Matthew and Luke, includes key details that the other lacks. The reasons, as Robb explains, have much to do with the original audiences for these Gospel writers, who emphasized parts of the story that would have the most meaning for their readers. Those differing emphases start at the very beginning, including the role of the angels, how they appeared, and to whom.

Most of all, Robb invites readers to lean in and consider not just what the angels say to the people they encounter in the Bible but what they may say to us today. As she shows throughout the book, messages from God require a response, and the Gospel writers wanted readers to find themselves in these stories of Jesus and his first followers. What response do the angels of Christmas ask of us? Where can we look for God's messengers today? How do we discern what they may be saying to us? And, having been entrusted with the message, how do we become the messengers to speak and act on God's behalf?

This leader guide is designed to help Christian adult education leaders guide a group through a four-session Advent study of the angels of Christmas, a study informed by Robb's book. The guide contains quotes from her book that can serve as prompts for discussion, but groups will gain the most when the guide is accompanied by reading *The Angels of Christmas*, the words of the prophets, and the Gospel narratives of Jesus's birth.

About the Sessions

Here is an overview of the four sessions in this leader guide:

- In Session 1, "Standing in the Presence of God: Gabriel and Zechariah," participants will connect the angels who appear in the Advent and Christmas stories to other stories of angels in the Bible, particularly the Old Testament, so they can more fully appreciate the reactions of the human beings to whom the angels appear. As background, they will also gain a greater understanding of why the Gospel writers (including the two who mention nothing of Jesus's birth) tell their stories the way they do, and with this background they will have a greater appreciation for the role of the angels in the Gospel accounts of Matthew and Luke. In studying the stories of John the Baptist's parents, Zechariah and Elizabeth, participants will examine their own responses to messages from God. They also will be able to connect the story of this couple, who had reached their older years without being blessed with children, to periods of spiritual barrenness in our own lives—and how God hears our prayers and remains with us throughout such times. Finally, this session will introduce participants to a theme that runs throughout *The Angels of Christmas*: that angels gather among us today, perhaps in forms we do not immediately recognize, and still bring us messages from God of hope, comfort, joy, and calling.
- In Session 2, "Let It Be: Gabriel and Mary," participants will connect Mary's encounter with the angel Gabriel to their own willingness to step out in faith amid situations

that may be uncertain or even frightening. They will gain a
deeper understanding of what it means to be willing vessels
for God's work in the world. In studying Mary's song of
praise, the Magnificat, they will connect Mary's experience
with Jesus's message, emphasized throughout Luke's Gospel,
that he came to lift up the lowly, and they will more fully
understand what Jesus meant in saying that he brought good
news to the poor.

- Session 3, "Acting on the Unbelievable: An Angel of the Lord
and Joseph," takes participants into the experience of Joseph,
who had three separate encounters with angels, including
two after Jesus was born. It also invites participants to put
themselves in Joseph's situation once he learns of Mary's
pregnancy, but before the first appearance of the angel to
him in a dream, and helps them better appreciate Joseph's
response to what he could only assume was a marriage-
breaking act of infidelity. With this in mind, participants
will recognize how Joseph, instead of ignoring the
commandments of the Law in this situation, actually acted
in keeping with the heart and spirit of the Law, presaging
Jesus's message that what God valued was mercy more than
sacrifices. Finally, participants will understand how Matthew,
writing to an audience of Jewish followers of Jesus, presents
Jesus's arrival as the fulfillment of Israel's traditions and
history, not some radical break with their experience of God.

- In Session 4, "Hark the Herald Angels Sing: The Angels and
the Shepherds," participants will place themselves in the
position of the shepherds who received a visitation from the
angels. They will appreciate why Luke alone chose to include
this story, and how angels' appearance and message near the
beginning of his Gospel helps establish one of the themes for
the arc of the story of Jesus's life and ministry. Then they will
consider how the shepherds responded to the news they had
received. Then, drawing on their reading of the epilogue to

The Angels of Christmas, they will recognize how angels can help sustain people through difficult circumstances—and will be able to see themselves in the role of human angels, messengers of God's love, hope, and steadfastness.

Each of the four session plans includes:

* stated goals for you to keep in mind as you lead discussions on the printed text from the New Revised Standard Version (NRSV) selections of Jesus's words from the cross discussed in that session (sessions contain additional Scripture texts as well, and all sessions refer participants to other passages in several discussion questions)
* extensive discussion questions to facilitate participants' engagement with both the biblical text and *The Angels of Christmas* book (you likely won't have time or desire to use all of the questions; choose the ones most interesting or relevant to your group)
* opening and closing prayers to ground your sessions in an atmosphere of worship

Some sessions contain optional easy-to-prepare and easy-to-do activities to serve as icebreakers or interactive introductions to the session's topic. Each session's Leader Preparation notes will alert you to any extra materials you need or preparation to accomplish.

Leading Virtual Small-Group Sessions

Meeting online is a great option for a number of situations. During a public-health hazard, such as the COVID-19 pandemic, online meetings are a welcome opportunity for people to converse while seeing each other's faces. Online meetings can also expand the "neighborhood" of group members because people can log in from just about anywhere in the world. Online gatherings also give those who do not have access to transportation or who prefer not to travel at certain times of day the chance to participate.

Introduction

The following guidelines will help you lead an effective and enriching group study using an online video conferencing platform.

Basic Features for Virtual Meetings

There are many choices for videoconferencing platforms. You may have personal experience and comfort using a particular service, or your church may have a subscription that will influence your choice. Whichever option you choose, you should use a platform that supports the following features:

- **Synchronous video and audio:** Participants can see and speak to one another in real time. They also have the ability to turn their video off and on and to mute and unmute their audio.
- **Chat:** Participants can send messages to the whole group or to individuals within the virtual meeting. Also, they can put active hyperlinks ("clickable" internet addresses) into the chat for other participants' convenience.
- **Screen sharing:** Participants can share the contents of their screens with other participants (the meeting host's permission may be required).
- **Video sharing:** Participants (or the host) can share videos and computer audio via screen share so that all participants can view each week's videos.
- **Breakout rooms:** Meeting hosts can automatically or manually send participants into virtual smaller groups, and they can determine whether or not participants will return to the main group automatically after a set period. Hosts can communicate with all breakout rooms. This feature is useful if your group is large or if you wish to break into teams of two or three for certain activities.

Check with your church administration to see if there is a preferred platform or an account that you might use. In most instances, only the host will need to be signed in to the account; others can participate without being registered.

Zoom, Webex, Google Meet, and Microsoft Teams all offer free versions of their platform to use if your church doesn't have an account. However, there may be restrictions (for instance, Zoom's free version limits meetings to forty-five minutes). Check each platform's website to be sure you are aware of any such restrictions before you sign up.

Once you have selected a platform, familiarize yourself with all of its features and controls so you can facilitate virtual meetings comfortably. The platform's website will have lists of features and helpful tutorials, and often third-party sites will have useful information or instructions as well.

In addition to videoconferencing software, it is also advisable to have access to slide-creation software, such as Microsoft PowerPoint or Google Slides. These can be used to prepare slides for screen sharing to display discussion questions, quotes from the study book, or Scripture passages. You can also create a document to share—just make sure the print size is easy to read.

Video Sharing

For a video-based study, it's important to be able to screen share your videos so that all participants can view them in your study session. The good news is, whether you have the videos on DVD or streaming files, it is possible to play them in your session.

All of the videoconferencing platforms mentioned in the previous section support screen sharing videos. Some have requirements for assuring that sound will play clearly in addition to the videos. Follow your videoconferencing platform instructions carefully and test the video sharing in advance to be sure it works.

If you wish to screen share a DVD video, you may need to use a different media player. Some media players will not allow you to share your screen when you play copyright-protected DVDs. VLC is a free media player that is safe and easy to use. To try this software, download at videolan.org/VLC.

What about copyright? DVDs like those you use for group study are meant to be used in a group setting "real time." That is, whether you meet in person, online, or in a hybrid setting, Abingdon Press encourages use of your DVD or streaming video.

What is allowed: streaming an Abingdon DVD over Zoom, Teams, or similar platform during a small group session.

What is not allowed: posting video of a published DVD study to social media or YouTube for later viewing.

If you have any questions about permissions and copyright, email permissions@abingdonpress.com.

Amplify Media. The streaming subscription platform Amplify Media makes it easy to share streaming videos for groups. When your church has an Amplify subscription, your group members can sign on and have access to the video sessions. With access, they can watch the video on their own ahead of your group meeting, watch it during your group meeting, or view the video again after the meeting. Thousands of videos are on AmplifyMedia.com; they are easy to watch anytime, anywhere, and on any device, from phones and tablets to Smart TVs and desktops.

Visit AmplifyMedia.com to learn more or call 1-800-672-1789, option 4, to hear about the current offers.

Communicating with Your Group

Clear communication with your small group before and throughout your study is crucial no matter how you meet, and it is doubly important if you are gathering virtually.

Advertising the study. Be sure to advertise your virtual study on your church's website and/or in its newsletter, as well as any social media that your church uses. Request that pastors or other worship leaders announce it in worship services.

Registration. Encourage people to register for the online study so you can know all participants and have a way to contact them. Ideally, you will collect email addresses for each participant so that you can send communications and links to your virtual meeting sessions. An event planning tool such as SignUpGenius makes this easy, and it gives you a database of participants and their email addresses.

Welcome email. Before your first session, several days in advance, send an email to everyone registered for the study, welcoming them to the group,

14

reminding them of the date and time of your first meeting, and including a link to join the virtual meeting. It's also a good idea to include one or two discussion questions to prime the pump for reflection and conversation when you gather.

If you have members without internet service, or if they are uncomfortable using a computer and videoconferencing software, let them know they may phone in to the meeting. Provide them the number and let them know that there is usually a unique phone number for each meeting.

Weekly Emails. Send a new email two or three days before each week's session, again including the link to your virtual meeting and one or two discussion questions to set the stage for discussion. Feel free to use any of the questions in the Leader Guide for this purpose. If you find a quote from the book that is especially meaningful, include this as well.

Facebook. Consider creating a private Facebook group for your small group. Here you can both have discussion and invite reflection between your weekly meetings. Each week, post one or two quotes from the study book along with a short question for reflection, and invite people to respond. These questions can come straight from the Leader Guide, and you can revisit the Facebook conversation during your virtual meeting.

You might also consider posting these quotes and questions on your church's Facebook page, inviting people in your congregation beyond your small group to join the conversation. This is a great way to let people know about your study and to invite them to join your next virtual meeting.

During Your Virtual Sessions

During your virtual sessions, follow these tips to be sure you are prepared and that everything runs as smoothly as possible.

- Familiarize yourself with the controls and features of your videoconferencing platform, using instructions or tutorials available via the platform's website or third-party sites.
- Be sure you are leading the session from a well-lit place in front of a background free from excessive distractions.

- As leader, log into the virtual meeting early. You want to be a good host who welcomes participants by name as they arrive. Logging in early also gives you time to check how you appear on camera, so you can make last-minute adjustments to your lighting and background if needed.

- During each session, pay attention to who is speaking and who is not. Because of video and audio lags as well as internet connections of varying quality, some participants may inadvertently speak over each other without realizing they are doing so. As needed, directly prompt specific people to speak if they wish (for example, "Alan, it looked like you were about to say something when Sarah was speaking").

- If your group is large, you may want to agree with members on a procedure for being recognized to speak (for example, participants might "raise hands" digitally or type "call on me" in the chat feature).

- Instruct participants to keep their microphones muted during the meeting to avoid extraneous noise that can interrupt discussion. This includes chewing or yawning sounds, which can be embarrassing. When it is time for discussion, participants can unmute themselves.

- Remember that some participants may wish simply to observe and listen—do not pressure anyone to speak.

- Always get your group's permission before recording your online sessions. While those who are unable to attend the meeting may appreciate the chance to view it later, respect the privacy of your participants.

In challenging times, modern technology has powerful potential to bring God's people together in new and nourishing ways. May such be your experience during this virtual study.

SESSION 1

STANDING IN THE PRESENCE OF GOD

Gabriel and Zechariah

Session Goals

This session's reading, discussion, reflection, and prayer will equip participants to:

- orient themselves to be more receptive to God's presence and purposes;
- understand why the various Gospel writers chose to tell the story of Jesus's birth and life in their own distinctive ways;
- understand that just as Elizabeth and others in the Bible experienced physical barrenness, we all go through spiritually barren times, and that God hears our prayers and remains with us throughout such times;
- be able to hear and experience God during times of silence in our lives;

- find their voices to speak to God's work in their lives and of the good news of the gospel; and
- to recognize the presence of angels gathering among us in ways that do not conform to our traditional image of what angels look like and how they behave.

Biblical Foundations

In the days of King Herod of Judea, there was a priest named Zechariah, who belonged to the priestly order of Abijah. His wife was a descendant of Aaron, and her name was Elizabeth. Both of them were righteous before God, living blamelessly according to all the commandments and regulations of the Lord. But they had no children, because Elizabeth was barren, and both were getting on in years.

Once when he was serving as priest before God and his section was on duty, he was chosen by lot, according to the custom of the priesthood, to enter the sanctuary of the Lord and offer incense. Now at the time of the incense offering, the whole assembly of the people was praying outside. Then there appeared to him an angel of the Lord, standing at the right side of the altar of incense. When Zechariah saw him, he was terrified; and fear overwhelmed him. But the angel said to him, "Do not be afraid, Zechariah, for your prayer has been heard. Your wife Elizabeth will bear you a son, and you will name him John. You will have joy and gladness, and many will rejoice at his birth, for he will be great in the sight of the Lord. He must never drink wine or strong drink; even before his birth he will be filled with the Holy Spirit. He will turn many of the people of Israel to the Lord their God. With the spirit and power of Elijah he will go before him, to turn the hearts of parents to their children, and the disobedient to the wisdom of the righteous, to make ready a people prepared for the Lord." Zechariah said to the angel, "How will I know that this is so? For I am an old man, and my wife is getting on in years." The angel replied, "I am Gabriel. I stand in the presence of God, and I have been sent to speak to you and to bring you this good news. But now, because you did not believe my words, which will be fulfilled in their time, you will become mute, unable to speak, until the day these things occur."

Meanwhile the people were waiting for Zechariah, and wondered at his delay in the sanctuary. When he did come out, he could not speak to them, and they realized that he had seen a vision in the sanctuary. He kept motioning to them and remained unable to speak. When his time of service was ended, he went to his home.

After those days his wife Elizabeth conceived, and for five months she remained in seclusion. She said, "This is what the Lord has done for me when he looked favorably on me and took away the disgrace I have endured among my people."

Luke 1:5-25

Suggested Leader Preparation

- Before your first session, set aside enough time to read Luke's account of the angel's visit to Zechariah and its aftermath, as contained in Luke 1. Read these passages in more than one translation (e.g., New Revised Standard Version, New International Version, New American Bible Revised Edition, The Message), including one you've never read before. Read these chapters aloud. Try summarizing the passage in your own words.

- As background, read the story of Hannah and the birth of Samuel, as contained in 1 Samuel 1:19–2:10. Again, try reading this passage in several translations. Make notes comparing Hannah's situation with that of Elizabeth, and note the responses of each woman to God's answer to their prayers.

- Carefully read *The Angels of Christmas* by Susan Robb, introduction and chapter 1. Note any material you need or want to research further before the session.

- Have on hand Bible dictionaries and concordances (and/ or identify trusted online equivalents), a variety of Bible translations for participants to use (recommended), and pencils/pens and paper. If you are in touch with the people likely to join you for these sessions, invite them to bring their own Bibles. *Optional:* Gather an assortment of recent newspapers and magazines.

- If using the DVD (also available as streaming video) in your study, preview the Session 1 segment and choose the best time in your session to view it.

As Your Group Gathers:
Orient the Study toward Advent and Angels

Welcome participants. Ask them to introduce themselves and to talk briefly about what they hope to gain from this study of Susan Robb's *The Angels of Christmas*. Be ready to talk about your personal interest in and hopes for the study as well. If no one mentions Advent specifically, ask participants why they chose to be part of an Advent study. Invite them to discuss various ways they have observed Advent, both personally and as part of a faith community. Note, as Robb does, that our word *Advent* comes from a word for "visitation," referring specifically to a visit by the emperor. Such a visit would require preparation by host communities, such as refurbishing dilapidated structures, new landscaping, and so on.

Ask:

- What preparations do you need to make for the arrival of the messiah?
- What "structures" need to be changed?
- How might you need to be spiritually "refurbished" to be ready for the Christ Child?

Emphasize that this is not only an Advent study; specifically, it is about the role of angels in the coming of the good news of Jesus—and in serving as messengers of God now as well as then. Note that while for us today Advent is about preparing our hearts for the arrival of the Messiah, for Elizabeth and Zechariah the message involved an unprecedented change in their life together; they weren't preparing to observe a season on the religious calendar but preparing to carry out a mission for God that involved shepherding a special child into and through the world.

Pray this prayer or one in your own words:

O God, at this time every year, we prepare ourselves in mind and spirit to be ready for the arrival of the Christ Child and what your remarkable intervention into human history meant and still means for our world. Kindle in us a spirit such that our preparations are not simply superficial, not simply going through the motions, not an observance that is reduced to nothing more than tradition. Just as we would make preparations for a special guest in our homes, help us change our hearts to make them a welcoming place where you can always stay. And help us to be more aware of and attentive to the messengers you send throughout our lives—the angels that are among us always. Amen.

Frame the Study Around Angels

In the introduction to her book, Susan Robb writes that "the angels in the stories of Jesus's birth are significant to our time of waiting and preparation in Advent." Discuss these questions:

- Based on your knowledge of the Bible and what you have read so far in *The Angels of Christmas*, how would you explain the role of the angels in the story of Jesus's coming?
- How does thinking of angels as messengers (the meaning of the word in Greek) contribute to your understanding of the role that angels play?

Discuss:

- Before you read the introduction and first chapter of *The Angels of Christmas*, what came to mind—images, actions, stories—when you thought of angels in the Bible?
- How did your perceptions evolve after reading the introduction and chapter 1?

- Invite participants to name all of the examples they can recall
  of appearances by angels in the Bible. For each example
  named, discuss the role the angel(s) played in these stories.
  Some examples to include, if participants do not mention
  them without prompting:
  ◊ the angels' appearance to Abraham and Sarah
    (Genesis 18:1-15)
  ◊ the angels' appearance to Hagar (Genesis 16:7-14)
  ◊ the angels' appearance to Jacob (Genesis 28:10-12)
  ◊ the angel's appearance to Moses (Exodus 3:1-4)
  ◊ the angels' appearance to Balaam (Numbers 22:31-35)
  ◊ the angel's appearance to Joshua (Joshua 5:13-15)
  ◊ an angel's message to the people (Judges 2:1-4)
  ◊ the angels' appearance to Gideon (Judges 6:11-24)
  ◊ the angel's appearance to Samson's mother (Judges 13:6-21)
  ◊ the angel sent to punish Jerusalem (2 Samuel 24:15-17)
  ◊ the angel's appearance to Daniel (Daniel 9:20-27)
  ◊ the angel's appearance to the prophet Zechariah
    (Zechariah 2:1-5)
  ◊ the angel's appearance to women at the tomb
    (Matthew 28:2-7)
  ◊ the angels' appearance to Mary (John 20:11-13)
  ◊ the angels' appearance to the disciples (Acts 1:6-11)
  ◊ the angel sent to rescue Peter from jail (Acts 12:1-11)
  ◊ an angel's appearance to Philip (Acts 8:26)
  ◊ the angel's message to Cornelius (Acts 10:3-32)
  ◊ an angel's appearance to Paul (Acts 27:21-25)
  ◊ the angels' announcement to the world (Revelation 14:6-8)
- Name all of the movies, TV shows, or stories you can think of
  that involve angels. For each example named, ask participants
  to describe the role that the angels played in these stories. How
  do these examples from popular culture affect your perception
  of angels and their purpose? Compare and contrast these roles
  with those you named for angelic appearances in the Bible.

- Why do you think people are so fascinated by angels?
- Do you believe that angels are among us today?
  Why or why not?

Finding Holy Spaces and God's Presence

Susan Robb opens the chapter by describing a Christmas Eve service when, for her, the presence of God was palpable. When he encountered the angel Gabriel, Zechariah was performing his duties in the Temple, a place, as the house where God was believed to dwell, where one would expect to feel God's presence all around. The Bible tells us of people who have felt God's strong presence in certain places. Read together the story of Jacob at Bethel in Genesis 28:10-17. Discuss:

- Why do you believe there are certain times and places where people say they palpably feel God's presence?
- Describe times and places where you have felt God's presence strongly. What senses or emotions did you feel?
- What do you think creates opportunities for feeling God's presence? Does it have more to do with the place and time, or with you?
- Gabriel announces to a startled Zechariah that he stands "in the presence of God" (Luke 1:19). Have you ever been in a situation when you felt that God was announcing God's presence? Describe the occasion.
- How do you think you would have responded, had you been in Zechariah's place, to the arrival of a being who stands in God's presence?
- How do you sense that someone speaks with spiritual authority from God?

Encountering an Angel

When the priest Zechariah goes to the Temple, he knows he has been chosen for a special duty, but he has no idea that he will be confronted by the angel Gabriel. From Scripture and tradition, Zechariah knows who Gabriel is, and to remove any doubt the angel identifies himself by name. But as Susan Robb suggests in *The Angels of Christmas*, people also sometimes encounter everyday angels, whose identity and purpose may not be clear to them in the moment.

Invite the participants to discuss these questions:

- Have you known others who believe they have been in the presence of angels? Or have you had such an experience yourself? Describe what it was like.
- How might you discern whether or not you had been in the presence of an angel? How would you discern what a message from the angel meant?
- Had you been in Zechariah's position, how do you think you would have reacted to a visitation from a being who identified himself (or herself) as an angel and told you that you were about to play a part in God's larger plan?
- Why do you think the angel needs to reassure Zechariah that he shouldn't be afraid? Why might a priest who knows the Scriptures be afraid of an angel, whose existence he already accepts as a matter of faith?
- Luke wants us to know that "the whole assembly of the people"—a term used in the Old Testament to describe all of the tribes of Israel (see Deuteronomy 5:22; 1 Chronicles 29:10; 1 Kings 8:22)—is praying outside the Temple when Gabriel appears to Zechariah inside the sanctuary (Luke 1:10). Why do you think Luke includes this detail? What does it add to your understanding of who John was to be?

In the Presence of God

Use the questions below to lead participants in a discussion of Gabriel's statement that the prayer of Zechariah and all the people have been heard by God.

- How was God answering the prayers of the people in the birth of John the Baptist?
- Where today do you see occasions when people across a society are praying for something together?
- Why do we pray some prayers together as a congregation? How does praying for something as a group, compared to individual prayer, alter the experience for you?
- When have you seen "the prayers of the people" answered?
- If these prayers have not been answered, how does that affect your attitude toward common prayer?
- When have your prayers been answered that resulted in a blessing for others as well?

God of the Childless

In *The Angels of Christmas*, Susan Robb reminds us that the story of Zechariah and Elizabeth follows a familiar formula for readers of the Bible. It is so familiar, as she notes, that as soon as we read of this couple's childlessness, we can predict what is about to happen. As a prelude to a discussion about what their inability to have children together might have been a source of anxiety and suffering for Elizabeth and Zechariah, read the stories of others in the Bible who had been in similar situations. For the story of Abraham and Sarah, read together Genesis 11:30; 12:1-5; 17:1-2, 15-17; and 18:1-2, 9-14. For the story of Hannah: read 1 Samuel 1:1-2, 6-7, 9-11, 27-28; 2:1-10. Explain that in the time of Zechariah and Elizabeth, children were regarded as a blessing from God, and that a woman's status in society was confirmed if she produced children. Note particularly that first-century Judaism did not treat barrenness as punishment from God, nor was there any religious reason for a childless woman to feel shame or be ostracized. Nevertheless, as Robb points out, human beings on their own sometimes presume on God's behalf to impose judgments on others about suffering they have endured, such as the case of a child born with a disability or other congenital condition.

25

Ask:

- Have you ever known anyone who had been told that some type of personal or familial suffering was punishment for sin? Without naming anyone involved, describe the situation. How did it make you feel? How did you react?
- If there is no biblical basis for believing that childlessness (or some other congenital condition) reflects punishment from God for someone's sin, why do you think people express this belief and impose judgment on others? Why/how might people sometimes place blame upon themselves for an unfortunate, unavoidable situation?
- Can you think of societies and situations where a woman's primary role was to produce children (examples might include royal families, such as Princess Diana or the wives of Henry VIII)? In such societies, how might women feel that an inability to have children reflected a lack of blessing from God?
- Have you ever experienced a barrenness in your life (either physical or spiritual) that seemed as if it would never end— but by God's grace, it finally was replaced with joy?
- Read the story of Jesus's encounter with a man who had been blind from birth (John 9). Note that Jesus's own disciples assumed the man's condition was punishment for sin. How does Jesus redirect them? What do you think Jesus means in saying that this situation presents an opportunity to reveal "the glory of God"? How does his response provide a model for our own response to suffering in others?

Susan Robb notes that there are times in our lives when we experience "spiritual barrenness."

- How would you describe spiritual barrenness?
- Where do you sense God's presence during such times?
- How are you sustained by feelings of God's presence?

Optional Activity

Invite participants to use their cell phones to look up the meanings of their given names. Have them share their findings with the group. Then refer to the discussion in *The Angels of Christmas* regarding the instruction the angels give to Zechariah and Elizabeth that their child is to be named John. Explain that John derives from the Hebrew name *Yochanan*, which means "Yahweh is gracious." Discuss:

- How does John's name reflect God's work in the lives of John's family, his nation, and the wider world?
- If you were to be named in a way that was meant to reflect your mission and purpose in life, what would your name be? Building on your earlier cell phone search, choose an English word that reflects your mission; then search for names that convey the meaning of that word. Examples: Names that mean "love" include Rhys and Phillip (for boys) and Amanda and Mila (for girls).

Closing Activity

Remind participants that this is an Advent study—a time to prepare our hearts and minds for the coming of Christ. Just as we prepare our homes for the coming of special visitors, we should think of the imminent arrival of the Christ Child as a time for a spiritual housecleaning and getting our hearts ready to receive God in the person of a human being.

This is also, particularly, a study about angels and the role they play in both the Christmas story and in the ongoing story of our lives. A running theme in each chapter will be how angels are in our midst today.

At the end of each session, ask these two questions:

1. In the coming week, how will you prepare yourself to receive the Christ Child?
2. In the past week, where have you made a possible "angel sighting"?

Close the session with this prayer or one of your own:

Lord, this season reminds us that you came to dwell with us, not just as a visitor but to experience life as one of us and to live in our hearts forever. Help us to be welcoming hosts for you by seeing you in everyone we meet and treating each person as we would treat you. And help us not only to hear the message of the angels but to spread to others the message that they are important and they are loved. Amen.

LET IT BE

Gabriel and Mary

Session Goals

This session's reading, discussion, reflection, and prayer will equip participants to:

- reflect on the relationship between Mary and her older cousin Elizabeth and on what brought them together during their respective pregnancies;
- appreciate more fully Mary's acceptance of the angel's message and willingness to step out in faith;
- understand what it means for us to be willing vessels for God's work in the world;
- understand Luke's special concern for how the story of Jesus, beginning with the angel's appearance to Mary, represented good news to the poor;
- reflect on how voluntarily humbling ourselves in favor of those who are less fortunate can serve God's intention that all human beings be fully included in the "beloved community;"

- consider the possibility of angels in our midst today and how they serve as God's messengers; and
- understand our own calling to be messengers of God's good news to others—that is, to be angels.

Biblical Foundations

In the sixth month the angel Gabriel was sent by God to a town in Galilee called Nazareth, to a virgin engaged to a man whose name was Joseph, of the house of David. The virgin's name was Mary. And he came to her and said, "Greetings, favored one! The Lord is with you." But she was much perplexed by his words and pondered what sort of greeting this might be. The angel said to her, "Do not be afraid, Mary, for you have found favor with God. And now, you will conceive in your womb and bear a son, and you will name him Jesus. He will be great, and will be called the Son of the Most High, and the Lord God will give to him the throne of his ancestor David. He will reign over the house of Jacob forever, and of his kingdom there will be no end." Mary said to the angel, "How can this be, since I am a virgin?" The angel said to her, "The Holy Spirit will come upon you, and the power of the Most High will overshadow you; therefore the child to be born will be holy; he will be called Son of God. And now, your relative Elizabeth in her old age has also conceived a son; and this is the sixth month for her who was said to be barren. For nothing will be impossible with God." Then Mary said, "Here am I, the servant of the Lord; let it be with me according to your word." Then the angel departed from her.

Luke 1:26-38

Suggested Leader Preparation

- Carefully and prayerfully read this passage and make notes of whatever grabs your attention most and sparks questions or new insights. If desired, consult a trusted Bible commentary.
- Carefully read *The Angels of Christmas*, chapter 2. Note any material you need or want to research further before the session.

- Have on hand a variety of Bible translations and trusted study Bibles and commentaries for participants to use (recommended).
- If using the DVD, preview the Session 2 segment and choose the best time in your session to view it.

As Your Group Gathers

Welcome participants. Ask those who attended the previous session to talk briefly about what in it most interested, challenged, or helped them.

Note that this week's discussion centers around the life and feelings of a young girl, believed by most to have been a teenager, and perhaps as young as fourteen or fifteen. To better understand and appreciate how Mary responded to the angel, invite the group to spend a few moments in silence trying to recall their own early teenage years—how they felt about themselves and their place in their community, what fears or uncertainties they faced, the emotions they felt, their ideas about what the future might hold for them. Especially focus on memories of sudden changes to their lives, such as moving to a new community or the loss of someone important to them

Invite participants to share some of these recollections and feelings if they are comfortable in doing so.

Then say: "As you recall feelings and experiences from that time in your life, seeing the world again through the eyes of a teenager, perhaps it is easier to imagine what it must have been like for Mary. One day, she receives shocking news that she is told will change the world—and will, if true, undoubtedly change her own life forever. To prepare yourself for today's discussion, try to imagine what must have been going through Mary's mind, the jumble of thoughts and emotions, when a heavenly messenger intruded into her life. Imagine how you, as a teenager, would have responded to the kind of news the angel brought."

Pray this prayer or one in your own words:

Lord, none of us expects to be visited by the angel Gabriel. None of us expects to receive a world-changing message such as Mary received. But we know there are times when you call us to a role or a task that we did not expect, or for which we feel unprepared. Through your Spirit, open our hearts to new purposes and new beginnings. Help us to be receptive to the miraculous ways you work in our world, even as they lie beyond our ability to comprehend. Give us a spirit such that when you come to us, we may say as Mary said, "Let it be according to your word" and follow in faith where you lead us to go. Amen.

Mary and Elizabeth

After receiving the news from the angel about her pregnancy and that of Elizabeth, Mary sets off for an extended visit with her faraway cousin. Luke does not tell us specifically why Mary decided to make this trip; we can only speculate or make inferences about her reasons. Susan Robb suggests some of these possibilities in chapter 2. Maybe Elizabeth, as a trusted elder relative, was a person in whom Mary could confide and seek wise counsel. Maybe she wanted to confirm the angel's news about Elizabeth's pregnancy. Maybe it was more convenient for Mary not to be in Nazareth for a time, where her pregnancy might become a source of gossip. Or maybe Mary's thinking was that she and Elizabeth could provide mutual encouragement about what God was doing in their lives. Discuss these questions:

- Since we have no clear answer about why Mary made her trip, we can only suggest possibilities, and there are no definitive answers. Why do you think Mary went? What reasons make the most sense to you?
- Think of others in your own life to whom you could turn for counsel, emotional support, or just a sympathetic ear. Invite participants, as they are comfortable, to share with the group what that relationship meant to them—or share an experience of your own. How do these relationships give you added insights into what the relationship between Mary and Elizabeth might have meant to each of these women.

Why would the opportunity to be with Elizabeth have been good for Mary? How would being with Mary have been helpful for Elizabeth?

- How might spending several months with each other have helped Mary and Elizabeth experience God's presence more fully in their lives? How might it have helped prepare them not only for giving birth according to God's plan, but for the ongoing job of raising children who were dedicated for a special role in God's redemptive work for the world?

- Put yourself in the position of Mary and Elizabeth. How would you feel if you learned that you were to be the parent of a child destined for a special purpose for God? What thoughts would race through your head? Could you imagine feeling both excited and fearful at the same time?

How Can This Be? Let It Be!

Susan Robb describes Mary's perplexity at the angel's announcement that she is carrying a child who will be the Messiah, and she contrasts Mary's confused reaction with that of the older and more experienced Zechariah, whom, as Robb suggests, seems skeptical of the news he hears from Gabriel. By the end of the encounter, just a few verses later, Mary is ready, without hesitation, to embrace this new, perplexing, and perhaps daunting mission, as she responds to God's messenger: "Let it be with me according to your word" (Luke 1:38). Discuss these questions:

- Mary is usually presumed by scholars to be a young teenager. How do you think her age might have affected how she reacted to the angel's message?

- Thinking back to your own teenage years, how do you think you might have reacted to the sudden appearance and words of the angel?

- In chapter 2 of *The Angels of Christmas*, Susan Robb notes examples of other figures in the Bible who receive unexpected angelic visitors with surprising news from God, and she invites us to compare their reactions with that of Mary. Review these stories as a group as contained in Genesis 31:11 and 46:2 (Jacob); Exodus 3:4 (Moses); 1 Samuel 3:4 (Samuel); and Isaiah 6:8 (Isaiah). How does Mary's response compare to each of these figures? What did you notice about her response that stands out to you from that of the others?

- After dropping the amazing news that she is pregnant with a child who will be called "the son of the Most High," the angel gives Mary another piece of information: that her much older cousin Elizabeth, who lives some distance away in Judea, also is expecting a baby. The text does not make explicit why the angel tells Mary about Elizabeth, so we are left to work from interpretation and inference. Susan Robb suggests that Elizabeth's pregnancy—which is at that time six months along and physically evident—is presented to Mary as a sign that his words are trustworthy, since Mary apparently does not yet know of Elizabeth's situation. Based on your own reading and reasoning, why do you think the angel includes the news about Elizabeth? Consider as many possible reasons as may occur to you. What do the angel's words at the end of this passage—"For nothing will be impossible with God"—suggest to you about the angel's purpose (Luke 1:37)?

- Is there anything you sense God is calling you to do? Is there anything you sense God desires to give birth to in your life that could make a difference in the world around you? If so, what are the consequences and struggles you might face by answering, "Here am I, the servant of the Lord. Let it be with me according to your word"?

- What might be the honor in saying yes to God's desires?

Nothing Will Be Impossible

Susan Robb accentuates Mary's words—"How can this be?"—that reflect her puzzlement over the news she has just received from the angel. The main source of her cognitive dissonance seems to be that she is a virgin, as she specifically states. But there may be additional reasons for her confusion too. And, as Robb points out, we often react to startling news, such as the unexpected loss of a friend or loved acquaintance, by asking how this could happen, even if we intellectually understand what occurred. Discuss these questions:

- Besides her understanding of the physical impossibility that a virgin could become pregnant, what other reasons can you think of why Mary might have asked, "How can this be?"
- How might Mary's age and status have contributed to her puzzlement over why God had chosen her for the role of bringing the Christ Child into the world?
- The scriptures we call the Old Testament are filled with stories of seemingly unlikely people who were chosen by God for special roles. Invite the group to provide examples and describe why these individuals were unlikely choices (and often, themselves were utterly surprised to have been chosen). Some examples that may have been familiar to Mary include Abraham and Sarah (too old to have children, much less to begin a line whose descendants would someday be a nation); Moses (poor speaking skills, outlaw status in Egypt); Gideon (a fearful man from a small clan, hardly a "mighty warrior" to repel invading enemies); and David (young and unimposing). Why might these people also have been the perfect choices for the roles to which God called them? In what ways do you think that Mary, if a surprising choice, also turned out to be an ideal choice?
- As part of this discussion, read the accounts of the "calling stories" of Moses (Exodus 3:1-15); Gideon (Judges 6:11-24);

and David (1 Samuel 16:1-13). Discuss how each of these figures reacted to the news that God had chosen him. Compare and contrast their reactions with Mary's response to the angel's message that nothing would be impossible with God.

• Invite participants to offer examples from their own lives or experience of situations that showed that nothing is impossible for God. Ask: What can make it difficult for us to accept that for God all things are possible? How can we more fully embrace Mary's simple faith that enabled her to say to the impossible, "Let it be"?

My Soul Magnifies the Lord

In preparation for this discussion, as a group read aloud Mary's song, the Magnificat, recorded in Luke's gospel:

My soul magnifies the Lord,
and my spirit rejoices in God my Savior,
for he has looked with favor on the lowliness of his servant.
Surely, from now on all generations will call me blessed;
for the Mighty One has done great things for me,
and holy is his name.
His mercy is for those who fear him
from generation to generation.
He has shown strength with his arm;
he has scattered the proud in the thoughts of their hearts.
He has brought down the powerful from their thrones,
and lifted up the lowly;
he has filled the hungry with good things,
and sent the rich away empty.
He has helped his servant Israel,
in remembrance of his mercy,
according to the promise he made to our ancestors,
to Abraham and to his descendants forever.

Luke 1:46-56

Ask participants:

- How would you describe what it means to "magnify the Lord"?
- When have you felt like magnifying the Lord? Do you recall a time when you experienced emotions toward God that Mary reveals through her song? How did you respond to those emotions?
- Susan Robb suggests that if we're honest, it may make us uncomfortable to read some of Mary's words that praise God for scattering the proud, bringing down the powerful, and sending the rich away empty. Until you read those words in preparation for this session, were you aware (or had you remembered) that Mary had included this sentiment? Did reading her words make you uncomfortable? If so, how? What do you think Mary meant?
- Why might the wealthy and comfortable be less likely to see Jesus's actions and teaching as good news? How is it possible to bring good news to the poor without displacing the well-to-do?
- How, as Susan Robb suggests, might choosing to humble ourselves bring about God's justice?
- Mary's song foreshadows another event that is recorded only in Luke's Gospel—when Jesus begins his public ministry in his hometown of Nazareth by reading the words of Isaiah that include "He has anointed me to bring good news to the poor" (Luke 4:18-21). The passage Luke cites from Isaiah reads: "good news to the oppressed." Why do you think Luke places so much added emphasis on the poor, compared to the other Gospels (for example, only Luke gives us the parable of the rich man and poor Lazarus [Luke 16])? Only Luke presents two different occasions when Jesus explicitly stated that bringing good news to the poor was part of his mission as Messiah. How do you believe that Jesus's actions and teaching represented good news to the poor?

- How can your church community live more fully into this part of Jesus's mission? How can you personally be more involved in bringing good news to the poor? How would you be playing the role of an angel in doing this?

Angels in Our Midst

At the end of chapter 2, Susan Robb includes a personal story about a message of comfort and reassurance she received as a child from a stranger who served for her as an angel. Discuss:

- When have you received a message of reassurance or comfort from someone you didn't know or didn't expect? How did you process that experience in retrospect? Did you think that this person might have been serving as an angel—or was an actual angel? If so, why?

Optional Activity

Remind participants of Susan Robb's theme that angels gather in our midst, often in forms we do not recognize based on culturally influenced perceptions of what angels look like and do. Invite members of the group to think about "angel sightings" they have experienced, read about, or heard about from others. Ask them to share these stories with the group. Discuss particularly the angels' message, how the recipients understood it, and what it meant to the recipients and others.

At the end of each session going forward, ask participants to share their angel sightings from the past week.

Closing Activity

Remind participants of one of the themes of this Advent study—that messages from God, such as those delivered by the angels of Christmas, require a response. Ask these questions:

- In the coming week, how will you prepare yourself to receive the Christ Child?

- In the coming week, how will you be more watchful for messages from God?
- Where do you believe God may have been at work to send a message to which you have not yet responded?
- How will you be more willing, in response to messages from God, to step out with the faith of Mary and say, "Let it be"?

Remind participants of John Wesley's famous prayer, known as the Wesleyan covenant prayer, which contains strong echoes of Mary's response to the angels. According to Wesley's journal, the prayer was first recited in London in 1755, at a service attended by eighteen hundred people in the Methodist movement. The words are understood as a response to God's grace at work in our lives—our obligations, as Wesley put it, in "renewing the covenant with God."

Close this session by inviting participants to pray these words together, in the accepting and faithful spirit of the teenage girl who carried Jesus into the world of human beings:

I am no longer my own, but thine.
Put me to what you wilt, rank me with whom thou wilt;
Put me to doing, put me to suffering.
Let me be employed by thee or laid aside for thee,
exalted for thee or brought low by thee;
Let me be full, let me be empty,
Let me have all things, let me have nothing:
I freely and heartily yield all things
to thy pleasure and disposal.
And now, O glorious and blessed God,
Father, Son and Holy Spirit,
thou are mine and I am thine. So be it.
And the covenant which I have made on earth,
let it be ratified in heaven. Amen.

SESSION 3

ACTING ON THE UNBELIEVABLE

An Angel of the Lord and Joseph

Session Goals

This session's reading, discussion, reflection, and prayer will equip participants to:

- see Jesus's arrival as the fulfillment and embodiment of Israel's traditions and history;
- recognize the presence of angels in our midst;
- have faith during trying times and situations;
- practice mercy as the heart of the Law;
- protect the Christ Child who is born in our hearts; and
- act in response to God's call upon their lives.

Biblical Foundations

Now the birth of Jesus the Messiah took place in this way. When his mother Mary had been engaged to Joseph, but before they lived together, she was found to be with child from the Holy Spirit. Her husband Joseph, being a righteous man and unwilling to expose her to public disgrace, planned to dismiss her quietly. But just when he had resolved to do this, an angel of the Lord appeared to him in a dream and said, "Joseph, son of David, do not be afraid to take Mary as your wife, for the child conceived in her is from the Holy Spirit. She will bear a son, and you are to name him Jesus, for he will save his people from their sins." All this took place to fulfill what had been spoken by the Lord through the prophet:

> *"Look, the virgin shall conceive and bear a son,*
> *and they shall name him Emmanuel,"*

which means, "God is with us." When Joseph awoke from sleep, he did as the angel of the Lord commanded him; he took her as his wife, but had no marital relations with her until she had borne a son; and he named him Jesus.

Matthew 1:18-25

Suggested Leader Preparation

- Carefully and prayerfully read Matthew 1:18-25, making notes of whatever grabs your attention most, sparks new questions, or prompts new insights. If desired, consult a trusted Bible commentary.
- Carefully read *The Angels of Christmas*, chapter 3. Note any material you need or want to research further before the session.
- Have on hand a variety of Bible translations and trusted study Bibles and commentaries for participants to use (recommended). You will need at least two different translations of Matthew 1:18-25.

- If using the DVD, preview the Session 3 segment and choose the best time in your session to view it.

As Your Group Gathers

Welcome participants. Ask those who attended the previous session to talk briefly about what in it most interested, challenged, or helped them.

As a way of leading them into this session, invite participants to think about three words—disgrace, betrayal, and mercy—that figure into the story related by Susan Robb in chapter 3 of *The Angels of Christmas*. As Robb points out, Joseph may well have felt betrayed by Mary when he learned of her unexpected pregnancy. Ask participants to look up various definitions of the word *betrayal* and share them with the group. Then invite them to think of a time when they felt betrayed. Drawing on these memories, ask them to suggest the emotions Joseph might have been feeling at the time, before the angel came to him in a dream. Discuss:

- What do you think you would have done in Joseph's place? Why?

Now consider the word *disgrace*. Remind participants that Joseph had concluded he did not want to expose Mary to "public disgrace" by calling attention to her out-of-wedlock pregnancy and shaming her before the community. Note that other translations say that Joseph did not wish to make a "public example" of Mary. Discuss these questions:

- How do you define "public disgrace"?
- What does it mean to make a public example of someone?
- What does it mean to face public disgrace today? What means do people use to try to make public examples of others in our society?
- How does the modern idea of "cancel culture" contribute to your understanding of Joseph's situation?

Invite participants to offer definitions for the word *mercy*. As Susan Robb notes, Jesus reminds the religious teachers of the words of the prophet

Hosea, who said that God desires mercy and not sacrifice—and then tells the Pharisees to go and study what that phrase means. Ask participants:

- You've just been given the same assignment by Jesus. To you, what does it mean that God desires mercy and not sacrifice?

Pray this prayer or one in your own words:

Lord, we have all experienced feelings of betrayal, disappointment with others, and anger. We have all experienced times of doubt and confusion, when we don't know what you want us to do. Remind us this week, and every week, that you are always with us and that you continually place your messengers in our midst. Help us to be awake to their presence and attentive to their message. And help us to be like Joseph, who believed what seemed unbelievable and acted decisively in response to your angels. Amen.

Prophecy Fulfilled

As Susan Robb points out, Matthew tells us no fewer than twelve times of an event in Jesus's story that served to fulfill what God had spoken, either directly or through prophets, in Hebrew scriptures. It begins with the visitation of the angel to Joseph. The angel quotes from Isaiah:

*"Look, the virgin shall conceive and bear a son,
and they shall name him Emmanuel,"*

which means, God is with us.

As Robb notes, the passage (Isaiah 7:14) refers to an event several centuries before Jesus, but Matthew uses it to show us that Isaiah's words speak to the situation in his day too—and that Jesus represents the fulfillment of the Law and the Prophets.

- Each week during Advent we light a candle with a special meaning. The third week of Advent is the candle of hope. How does the text for this lesson, in which the angel reveals God's plan to Joseph, illustrate hope?

Look up some other passages that Matthew cites as fulfillment of the Scriptures.

- Matthew 2:13-15
- Matthew 2:17-18
- Matthew 3:15
- Matthew 4:14
- Matthew 5:17
- Matthew 8:17
- Matthew 12:17
- Matthew 13:14
- Matthew 27:9
- Matthew 27:46

Ask:

- How might Christians interpret each of these passages to show that Jesus was the fulfillment of the Law and the Prophets?
- Why do you think Matthew, above all of the other Gospel writers, goes to such lengths to demonstrate this point for readers?
- How is Matthew's point emphasized by showing that the message about fulfillment of prophecy came from the angel?

The Heart of the Law

As Susan Robb points out in chapter 3 of *The Angels of Christmas*, Joseph faced a dilemma before the angel's appearance to him in a dream. He knew of Mary's pregnancy, and he knew that he was not the father. He didn't want to expose Mary to "public disgrace," as Matthew's text puts it (1:19). Under the Law, however, infidelity was grounds for divorce. Stoning was prescribed as a punishment, although there is no evidence from Old Testament times that this punishment was ever used. Because John's Gospel records a unique story of Jesus's response to an attempt to stone a woman caught in adultery, many Christians assume that this harsh, legalistic punishment reflected the prevailing mindset in first-century Judaism. But Robb directs us to look at other sources within Judaism, notably the prophet Hosea, whose wife actually did commit adultery. Twice in Matthew's Gospel—our only source for the Joseph stories—Jesus echoes Hosea 6:6 ("I desire steadfast love and not sacrifice") when he says, "I desire mercy, not sacrifice" (9:13, 12:7). As Robb notes, this message reflects the heart and spirit of the Law, and time and again in his ministry, Jesus directs people to follow the spirit of the Law, reflected in the commands to love God and love neighbor, above all. You may wish to offer this as background to participants to lead them into the following questions:

- Susan Robb invites us to imagine what is going through Joseph's mind as he learns of Mary's pregnancy. Putting yourself in Joseph's position, what do you think his concerns might have been? How might he have chosen to deal with those concerns in ways that were different from the course he had decided to take before the angel's appearance?

- In the United States, news of an out-of-wedlock pregnancy once would have been a source of scandal and gossip. How does this knowledge shed light on the situation in which Mary and Joseph found themselves?

- Based on what you have read so far in *The Angels of Christmas*, how does Joseph's choice to "dismiss Mary quietly," rather than shame her publicly, reflect the Law and the Hebrew Scriptures? How does Joseph's action add insight to the words of Hosea quoted by Jesus?

- Based on what Robb reveals to us about Matthew's audience and purpose, why do you think Matthew wants us to know about how Joseph resolved to deal with the dilemma of Mary's surprising pregnancy? Why might this story have resonated strongly with Matthew's Jewish Christian readers, who saw the growing split between Judaism and their new faith and worried that their old traditions and beliefs would be discarded?

- How does Joseph's merciful attitude toward Mary's pregnancy reflect attitudes Jesus will later show toward others?

Acting in Response to Angels

Say: "A running theme in Robb's *The Angels of Christmas* is the invitation to recognize how angels might appear to us today—and to discern what they are saying to us on God's behalf and how we should respond." Raise this theme in discussing these questions about Joseph's response to the angels.

- All of the figures in the first two chapters of this book— Zechariah, Elizabeth, and Mary—have been in the physical presence of angels. As we will see in chapter 4, the shepherds see and hear from angels in their presence. Joseph is the outlier. His angelic visitations occur in dreams. Would you be likely to interpret it differently if you encountered an angel in a dream instead of during your waking hours? Why or why not?
- What does it say to you about Joseph that he acted on the angels' messages—not just once but three times?
- Compare and contrast Joseph's faith response to that of Mary.
- What do the responses of Jesus's earthly parents suggest to you about the kind of household in which Jesus was raised?
- Do you believe it is possible that an angel would appear to you in some way other than physical form? How would you recognize what transpired as a message from God? How would you respond?
- What would lead you, in Susan Robb's word, to "act on the unbelievable"?
- As you consider this question, invite others to share stories of moments when they believe they were in the presence of an angel who took some form other than what traditional depictions might have led them to expect.

- Revisit the story of the angel in the red bandana. Why did so many people led to safety by this young man believe they had been visited by an angel? What, in your mind, defines the work of angels?
- What angels in your life have brought you protection?

Protecting the Christ Child

Susan Robb invites us to consider how the Christ Child is born not only into the world but into each of us. She notes all of the forces in our world that threaten to destroy the light of Christ. Then she asks us to put ourselves in the position of Joseph, who acted to protect the holy child in response to an angel's messages. Discuss these questions as a group:

- How might you seek to protect the Christ Child born in you this Advent season? Where do you see threats to the light of Christ?
- Susan Robb invites us to think about Jesus, Mary, and Joseph as refugees. How does their story help you relate to the situations faced by displaced persons today? What does Matthew want us to understand about Herod in Jesus's day—and the Herods of our own time?
- In what ways have you contributed to threatening that One born to you?
- How have you protected his presence in your life in the past?
- How do you see yourself and your church community bringing transformation to the world?

Optional Activity

In conjunction with the discussion of "the heart of the Law," read together Hosea 6:4-6. Then read two stories about Jesus's encounters with women described as sinful: Luke 7:36-50 and John 8:1-11. Discuss these questions:

- How do Jesus's responses to these women reflect Hosea's understanding of the heart of the Law?

48

- Why do you think the Gospel writers included these stories (each is unique to its particular Gospel) in what they wanted us to know about Jesus?
- Where do you see conflicts today among Christians between what they perceive as the rules of the law versus the spirit of the law?
- How do the above passages, and the story of Joseph's attitude toward Mary's pregnancy, contribute to your views on questions dividing Christians today?
- In your mind, is it possible to distinguish between the letter of the law and the spirit of the law? Explain.

Closing Activity

As Matthew's readers would have understood, Joseph was not the first person in Israel's history to have encountered God or God's messengers in a dream—and not the first to have had such an encounter at a time beset by worry and confusion. We can turn all the way back to Genesis, where we find two stories of Jacob. His first encounter comes after he leaves home, fleeing for his life from the anger of his brother, Esau (Genesis 28:10-17). Years later, when he at last returns to Canaan to face Esau, he again finds himself in the presence of a mysterious being, who gives him a new name: Israel.

Read these two passages as a group:

Jacob left Beer-sheba and went toward Haran. He came to a certain place and stayed there for the night, because the sun had set. Taking one of the stones of the place, he put it under his head and lay down in that place. And he dreamed that there was a ladder set up on the earth, the top of it reaching to heaven; and the angels of God were ascending and descending on it. And the Lord stood beside him and said, "I am the Lord, the God of Abraham your father and the God of Isaac; the land on which you lie I will give to you and to your offspring; and your offspring shall be like the dust of the earth, and you shall spread abroad to the west and to the east and to the north and to the south; and all the families of the earth shall be

49

blessed in you and in your offspring. Know that I am with you and will keep you wherever you go, and will bring you back to this land; for I will not leave you until I have done what I have promised you." Then Jacob woke from his sleep and said, "Surely the Lord is in this place—and I did not know it!" And he was afraid, and said, "How awesome is this place! This is none other than the house of God, and this is the gate of heaven."

Now have another member of the group read Genesis 32:9-12, 22-24, 26-30.

And Jacob said, "O God of my father Abraham and God of my father Isaac, O Lord who said to me, 'Return to your country and to your kindred, and I will do you good,' I am not worthy of the least of all the steadfast love and all the faithfulness that you have shown to your servant, for with only my staff I crossed this Jordan; and now I have become two companies. Deliver me, please, from the hand of my brother, from the hand of Esau, for I am afraid of him; he may come and kill us all, the mothers with the children. Yet you have said, 'I will surely do you good, and make your offspring as the sand of the sea, which cannot be counted because of their number.'"...

The same night he got up and took his two wives, his two maids, and his eleven children, and crossed the ford of the Jabbok. He took them and sent them across the stream, and likewise everything that he had. Jacob was left alone; and a man wrestled with him until daybreak.... Then he said, "Let me go, for the day is breaking." But Jacob said, "I will not let you go, unless you bless me."....And there he blessed him. So Jacob called the place Peniel, saying, "For I have seen God face to face, and yet my life is preserved."

Invite them to respond to these questions:

- Like Jacob, Joseph experienced God's presence in an unusual way—in Joseph's case, a dream. When have you experienced God's presence in an unusual way?
- Did this encounter leave you questioning whether the experience was real? How did you respond?

- Where in the coming week will you be more attentive to the possibility that God is trying to communicate with you?
- Jacob's second encounter with God or a heavenly being is life-changing; he emerges with a new name that means "the one who struggles with God." When have you had a life-changing encounter with God? How have you wrestled with God?
- How does Jacob's experience help you better understand the faith and response of Joseph to the message of the angels? How does it help you consider your own response to messages from God?

At the end of each session, ask these two questions:

1. In the coming week, how will you prepare yourself to receive the Christ Child?
2. In the past week, where have you had a possible "angel sighting"?

Close this session by praying these words or some of your own:

O God, we long for you to come to us, to be with us, and to speak to us. But we don't always recognize the occasions when you are sending your messengers to us, and we may find it easy to do nothing rather than to act in faith on the word you give to us. Help us to be inspired by the example of your servant, Joseph, who had the faith to believe and to act without hesitation, even when the message from your angels seemed unbelievable. Amen.

SESSION 4

HARK THE HERALD ANGELS SING

The Angels and the Shepherds

Session Goals

This session's reading, discussion, reflection, and prayer will equip participants to:

- place themselves in the position of the shepherds who received a visitation from the angels;
- appreciate why Luke chose to include the story of the shepherds and how their visitation from the angels near the beginning of his Gospel helps establish a theme for the arc of the story of Jesus's life and ministry;
- respond to the angels' messages to proclaim the good news, especially to the have-nots in our society; and
- recognize how angels can serve not only as heralds of news that brings great joy but as godly presences that help sustain people through difficult circumstances.

Biblical Foundations

In those days a decree went out from Emperor Augustus that all the world should be registered. This was the first registration and was taken while Quirinius was governor of Syria. All went to their own towns to be registered. Joseph also went from the town of Nazareth in Galilee to Judea, to the city of David called Bethlehem, because he was descended from the house and family of David. He went to be registered with Mary, to whom he was engaged and who was expecting a child. While they were there, the time came for her to deliver her child. And she gave birth to her firstborn son and wrapped him in bands of cloth, and laid him in a manger, because there was no place for them in the inn.

In that region there were shepherds living in the fields, keeping watch over their flock by night. Then an angel of the Lord stood before them, and the glory of the Lord shone around them, and they were terrified. But the angel said to them, "Do not be afraid; for see—I am bringing you good news of great joy for all the people: to you is born this day in the city of David a Savior, who is the Messiah, the Lord. This will be a sign for you: you will find a child wrapped in bands of cloth and lying in a manger." And suddenly there was with the angel a multitude of the heavenly host, praising God and saying,

> *"Glory to God in the highest heaven,*
> *and on earth peace among those whom he favors!"*

Luke 2:1-14

Suggested Leader Preparation

- Carefully and prayerfully read Luke 2:1-14, making notes of whatever grabs your attention most, sparks new questions, or prompts new insights. If desired, consult a trusted Bible commentary.
- Carefully read *The Angels of Christmas,* chapter 4. Note any material you need or want to research further before the session.

- Have on hand a variety of Bible translations and trusted study Bibles and commentaries for participants to use (recommended).
- If using the DVD, preview the Session 4 segment and choose the best time in your session to view it.
- Read some background on the role of shepherds in the society of Jesus's day.

As Your Group Gathers

Welcome participants. Ask those who attended the previous session to talk briefly about what in it most interested, challenged, or helped them.

In preparation before this session, search Google images for "paintings of the shepherds and the angels." You will find a number of representations, from medieval to modern times, of the scene of the army of angels appearing to the shepherds. Select five or six of these images and save them to a laptop or cell phone.

As an opening activity, say: "For centuries, artists have imagined what it must have been like for shepherds spending the night in an open field with their flock to have suddenly witnessed a multitude of angels in the sky—angels who brought them astonishing news. As you view a few of these images, try imagining with the artists what this experience must have been like. Put yourself in the place of these shepherds, ordinary workers going about their daily routine. Imagine your initial surprise and the mixture of awe, fear, and joy at what you saw in the night sky and the news you have just heard from the angels."

One by one, display the various images you have selected as the participants watch in silence, absorbing the range of emotions you have described.

After you have displayed the images, say: "As you put yourself in the place of these shepherds, ask yourself: 'Why did God's angels choose me, nobody special, nobody who would carry any weight with the powerful people in my society, to be the first to receive the most amazing news the world had ever heard?'"

Pray this prayer or one of your own:

Lord, as we prepare our hearts and minds during this Advent season, give us the spirit of the shepherds who first heard the news of Jesus's birth. Reanimate our sense of wonder and amazement at what you have done for us. And grant us the courage to find our voices and pass along, not just through our words but especially through our actions, the good news of great joy that your angels delivered for all humankind. Amen.

They Were Terrified

Using the questions that follow, guide your group in a discussion of how difficult times also create new possibilities for growth and change. If you have a large group, consider forming smaller teams to discuss these questions, and then have one person from each group bring the points or examples raised in their conversation back to the larger group.

- Why do you think the shepherds were afraid at the appearance of the angels? Why do you think the angels deemed it necessary in their encounters with Mary, Joseph, Elizabeth, Zechariah, and, later, the women who came to the tomb on Easter morning, to reassure them that they need not be afraid?
- Why do you think our initial impulse to something unexpected is fear? How is that impulse helpful? How can it be harmful?
- Can you think of a time when you were terrified to receive news that turned out to be good? Describe it.
- How can fear hold us back from experiencing something new and amazing?

As you have time, read the story of Jesus's raising of Lazarus in John 11—a chapter that in many ways is about fear in the face of the unknown. After reading this long passage, ask participants about the fears evidenced by various characters in the story:

- the disciples
- Martha
- the religious leaders in Jerusalem

Ask:

- What were they afraid of?
- How did their fears hold them back?

An Unexpected Christmas

Using the following questions, guide your group in a discussion of the amazing, unexpected experience of Mary and Joseph.

- In chapter 4 of *The Angels of Christmas*, Susan Robb describes a Christmas that was what her family had neither hoped for nor planned—a Christmas that involved an emergency appendectomy for her daughter—and how in spite everything, they found peace and experienced God's presence amid the turbulence. When have you experienced a Christmas where nothing seemed to unfold as you had imagined? Where, in the midst of it all, were you able to feel God's presence?
- Read the story of Joseph's reunion with his brothers, who had sold him into slavery (Genesis 45:1-15). Though the brothers had never imagined what would happen, Joseph wound up, through God's hand, in a position to save the family when a famine struck the land of Canaan. In one of the most memorable passages of the Bible, Joseph reveals himself to his brothers and tells them that what they had intended as evil, God had repurposed so that good could emerge. Have you ever experienced a situation where something hurtful or evil that was done to you ultimately ended in good? Where did you feel God's hand in these events? How can you relate Joseph's story to Robb's story of her unexpected Christmas? How did Mary and Joseph demonstrate faith before, during, and after their arduous journey to Bethlehem?

- Put yourself in the position of Mary and Joseph after the magi and the shepherds had departed—a moment that Robb suggests for us in chapter 4. What do you think they might have said to each other as they reflected on what had happened? How could they have related their experience in Bethlehem to the messages they had separately received from the angels? What would you have said in their position?

- As Susan Robb notes, the moment the angel revealed to Mary that her child would be called the Son of God, she would have known there would be conflict with the ruling powers representing the Roman emperor, who also had been proclaimed as the son of a god. How might Mary's experience with the angel, and with the arrival of visitors to the manger, have prepared her to be mother to a child who was destined for conflict?

- Throughout the book, Robb reminds us that the creche ultimately leads to the cross. Mary is the one figure whom the Gospels record being with Jesus in both places. How do you think her experience with the angel and her miraculous pregnancy might have prepared her to stay with Jesus through the end?

The Shepherds and the Angels

As Susan Robb explains, the Bible contains many references to sheep and shepherds across Israel's history. Read a few of these passages together.

- 1 Samuel 17:34-36
- Psalm 23
- John 10:11-16
- Genesis 48:15
- Revelation 7:17
- Isaiah 53:6

Discuss:

- How do these passages contribute to your understanding of the role and reputation of shepherds in the life of Israel?
- How did shepherds hold a special position? How did they hold a lowly position?
- How does Jesus's comparison of himself to a shepherd help you better understand why the angels first delivered the news of Jesus's birth to the shepherds near Bethlehem? How does it help you better understand the role that the angels entrusted to these shepherds to be the first evangelists to spread this good news?
- Have you ever thought of the shepherds, who routinely slept in open fields under the stars, as people without homes? How does thinking of them in this way give added meaning to God's choice to deliver the message of the arrival of the Savior of the world to a group of homeless men?
- In Luke's Gentile-dominated world, many on the lower rungs of the status-conscious Roman society—particularly slaves and women—were attracted to the message that in the body of Christ there were no distinctions between rich and poor, enslaved and free, male and female. How might Luke's inclusion of the shepherds near the beginning of his Gospel have helped draw the have-nots to these early Christian communities?
- Imagine that Jesus was born in this current season, and that God sent angels to herald his birth. Who would be the shepherds if Jesus were born today? Knowing what you know about the shepherds, what do you think the occupation of these modern recipients of the angels' message would be? Explain your answer.
- Have you ever witnessed something so wonderfully amazing that you had to tell others right away? Describe the experience. How did it make you feel to share this

news? What emotions ran through your mind? Relate your experience to that of the shepherds.

- Have you ever been delegated as a messenger to deliver important news to someone? How did you feel in being tasked with this responsibility? How can you relate this to the shepherds' experience after their encounter with the army of angels?

Being an Angel

In the epilogue to *The Angels of Christmas*, and elsewhere in the book, Susan Robb describes several occasions when angels brought not good news that created great joy and celebration but good news that sustained people through a dark and difficult time. For each of these occasions, briefly discuss how the message of the "angel" helped someone through a trying time:

- George Bailey, the character played by James Stewart in *It's a Wonderful Life*
- Susan Robb, whose friend brought her a needlepoint pillow after Robb's father died
- the childless couple depicted in the movie *Grand Canyon*
- the German pastor and political prisoner Alfred Delp

Next, turn to these questions:

- Why might the angels in each of these stories be regarded as a guardian angel?
- What does it mean to be a guardian?
- How are you as a Christian called to be a guardian for others? What is it that you are helping to "guard"?
- How does understanding your role as a guardian connect to Martin Luther King's statement that we are connected by "an inescapable network of mutuality"?
- Susan Robb writes of "long-term angels" who can produce a lasting impact on our lives or the lives of others over time.

Have you ever regarded angels in this way, as opposed to
those who make a dramatic, one-time appearance? Who
would you consider to be a longtime angel? Why?

- In both the introduction and the epilogue to *The Angels of
Christmas*, Susan Robb calls our attention to the enduring
presence of angels in movies and TV shows and other forms
of popular culture. In the Gospel stories, angels bring news
of joy: that Elizabeth and Zechariah at long last will be
blessed with a child; that God has lifted up the poor and
meek like Mary; that the Messiah has been born; and that
the crucified Jesus has been raised from the dead. Think
back on movies and TV shows that you have seen involving
angels. Have you ever noticed that in popular culture, angels
tend to fill a different role—that instead of bringing joy, they
bring comfort during difficult times and shepherd people
through danger? Or they look out for people who need a
helping hand that society doesn't seem inclined to give them?
Why do you think that in our culture's "angel stories" we
tend to gravitate toward this role for angels? What does this
reveal about how we see God working in our world? What
does it suggest about the role that God wants us to play as
messengers of God's love and comfort?

- Think back to the meaning of the word *Advent* noted in
the introduction. How does fulfilling the role of an angel
in someone's life prepare your heart for a visitation from the
King? How does it help prepare the way for the arrival of
God's kingdom?

Optional Activity

Because chapter 4 of *The Angels of Christmas* is bookended with a
description of *A Charlie Brown Christmas*, you may wish to play one or
more scenes for the group, particularly the final scene, in which Charlie
Brown returns to find that his classmates have decorated the scrawny tree.

61

(You can find this scene, and others from the original TV program, on YouTube.) Cue up the scene and watch it together on a laptop screen or video monitor. Discuss these questions after viewing:

- Upon watching this clip, did you notice anything that you had not seen on previous viewings? Explain.
- People relate to art and stories in their own ways. How does *A Charlie Brown Christmas* help you more fully understand what Christmas is all about?
- How does it help you follow the call during Advent to prepare your heart for the coming of Jesus?

To extend this activity, consider finding a small, spindly tree to bring to the session—or a small, metal tree or even a bare tree branch. Have Christmas decorations available. Invite participants to hang their decorations on your tree, as Charlie Brown's classmates did.

Say: "Remember, when you touch others with the good news of God's love for them, you are able to see them in a different light, and they are able to shine the way God intended."

After you are done decorating, take a photo with your cell phone of everyone gathered around the scrawny tree and share with the group.

Closing Activity

As you prepare to end this study, read together Isaiah 40:3-5.

A voice cries out:
"In the wilderness prepare the way of the Lord,
make straight in the desert a highway for our God.
Every valley shall be lifted up,
and every mountain and hill be made low;
the uneven ground shall become level,
and the rough places a plain.
Then the glory of the Lord shall be revealed,
and all people shall see it together,
for the mouth of the Lord has spoken."

Say: "Five hundred years before the birth of Jesus, the first readers of this passage from Isaiah understood it to mean that God was making a way through the impassible wilderness for the people to return home to Jerusalem from their exile in Babylon. Nineteen centuries after Jesus's lifetime, Martin Luther King Jr. quoted a verse from this passage in his famous 'I Have a Dream' speech to refer to the work ensuring civil rights for all. As Christians, we often read this passage during Advent to refer to the work of preparing the way for the coming of the Lord."

Discuss:

- What valleys need to be raised up, what crooked places need to be made straight, and what rough places need to be made smooth to "prepare the way of the Lord"?
- What will you do during this Advent season to prepare the way?

At the end of each session, ask these two questions:

- In the coming week, how will you prepare yourself to receive the Christ Child?
- In the past week, where have you had a possible "angel sighting"?

Pray this prayer or one of your own:

Lord, we remember how you sent your angels to bring the news of how you were working in our world. And we know that in Jesus you came to stay, that you are working each day to reveal your love for every last one of us. We know that you still work through angels in our midst, in ways we don't fully understand, and that sometimes you call on us to be your messengers who help people feel your presence. Help us to be faithful to that call and to your message so the good news of your rescuing and enabling love spreads like the light of the dawn onto a world where many still feel surrounded by darkness. Amen.

Printed in Great Britain
by Amazon

32370632R00036